P9-CRC-312

BLT
5/5/16
21.15

Families and their Faiths

Buddhism in Thailand

Written by Frances Hawker and Sunantha Phusomsai
Photography by Bruce Campbell

Crabtree Publishing Company
www.crabtreebooks.com

Crabtree Publishing Company

www.crabtreebooks.com

Authors: Frances Hawker and
    Sunantha Phusomsai
Editors: Su Swallow and Lynn Peppas
Proofreader: Crystal Sikkens
Editorial director: Kathy Middleton
Designer: Robert Walster, Big Blu Design
Photographs: Bruce Campbell
Artwork: Ketut Suardana
Production coordinator: Katherine Berti
Prepress technicians: Margaret Amy Salter
    and Katherine Berti

Frances Hawker and Bruce Campbell have traveled all around the world, beginning when they made their way overland from Europe to Australia thirty-five years ago. They have previously published ten children's books together.

Sunantha Phusomsai grew up in a small village in rural Thailand. She now lives in Bangkok with her husband and two children and is involved in taking computer access to remote parts of Thailand to increase education standards. She wanted to share her family's story, life, and religion through this book.

Library and Archives Canada Cataloguing in Publication

Hawker, Frances
    Buddhism in Thailand / Frances Hawker and Sunantha
Phusomsai ; photography by Bruce Campbell.

(Families and their faiths)
Includes index.
ISBN 978-0-7787-5006-2 (bound).--ISBN 978-0-7787-5023-9 (pbk.)

    1. Buddhism--Thailand--Customs and practices--Juvenile
literature. 2. Thailand--Religious life and customs--Juvenile
literature. I. Campbell, Bruce, 1950- II. Sunantha Phusomsai III.
Title. IV. Series: Hawker, Frances. Families and their faiths.

BQ566.H39 2009   j294.309593   C2009-902030-0

Library of Congress Cataloging-in-Publication Data

Hawker, Frances.
    Buddhism in Thailand / written by Frances Hawker and
Sunantha Phusomsai ; photography by Bruce Campbell.
        p. cm. -- (Families and their faiths)
    Includes index.
    ISBN 978-0-7787-5023-9 (pbk. : alk. paper)
-- ISBN 978-0-7787-5006-2 (reinforced library binding : alk. paper)
    1. Buddhists--Thailand--Juvenile literature. 2. Thailand--
Religious life and customs--Juvenile literature. I. Sunantha
Phusomsai. II. Campbell, Bruce, 1950- III. Title. IV. Series.

BQ566.H38 2009
294.309593--dc22

                                                    2009014156

Crabtree Publishing Company

www.crabtreebooks.com
1-800-387-7650

Published in Canada
Crabtree Publishing
616 Welland Ave.
St. Catharines, ON
L2M 5V6

Published in the United States
Crabtree Publishing
PMB16A
350 Fifth Ave., Suite 3308
New York, NY 10118

Contents

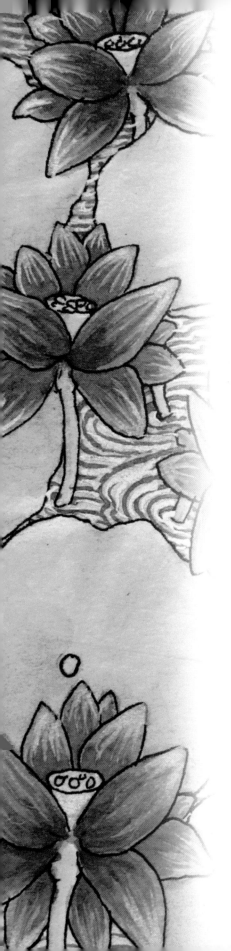

This is a story about my grandson, Baan.
He is eight years old. The **monks** came
today and asked him to become a monk.
Afterward, everyone watched the monks go.

"This brings us great honor, Baan. I'm very
proud of you," I say.

I am a rice farmer. I live in Thailand with
my wife and six grandchildren. Their parents
have gone to work in the city of Bangkok,
because there is no work for them here.

Baan and I go to the rice field to catch fish and frogs for dinner.

"Should I become a monk, Pa?" Baan asks.

"You are only a boy; you can decide later. When I was younger I became a monk for two years. Any time spent as a monk will help you in this life and your next one," I say.

Baan often helps the monks. He serves breakfast and does jobs at the **monastery**.

The monks are **Buddhists**. We are Buddhists too. We follow the Buddha's teachings. The **Buddha** is not a god. He was a prince in India more than 2,500 years ago.

8

Baan climbs into the rice barn to help me.

"I want to become a monk for the rainy season holidays to learn about Buddhism," Baan says.

"Your mother will be very proud. She has sent money to buy **offerings** for the monks. We will go to get them tomorrow," I say.

The next morning we go into town. Monks must not touch money, so they cannot go shopping. Baan chooses a bucket filled with rubber sandals, soap, toilet paper, and candles.

"What do the monks do with all these buckets?" laughs Baan.

Baan gets ready to become a monk for a few months. There will be a ceremony and he has a lot to learn. His cousins help him find a **lotus** leaf and three lotus flowers from the pond. The lotus is an important symbol in Buddhism. Like a perfect lotus flower growing from a muddy pond, an ordinary person can grow to become wise.

At last the day of the ceremony is here. The boys practice one last time. Then they ask their families to forgive them for any trouble they have caused in the past. They kneel on the ground and touch the floor three times with their heads.

The boys laugh and joke when their heads are shaved. Baan tries hard not to show he is nervous.

The hair falls onto the lotus leaf. This is a symbol for letting go of belongings. The boys then float the leaves on the water and make a wish.

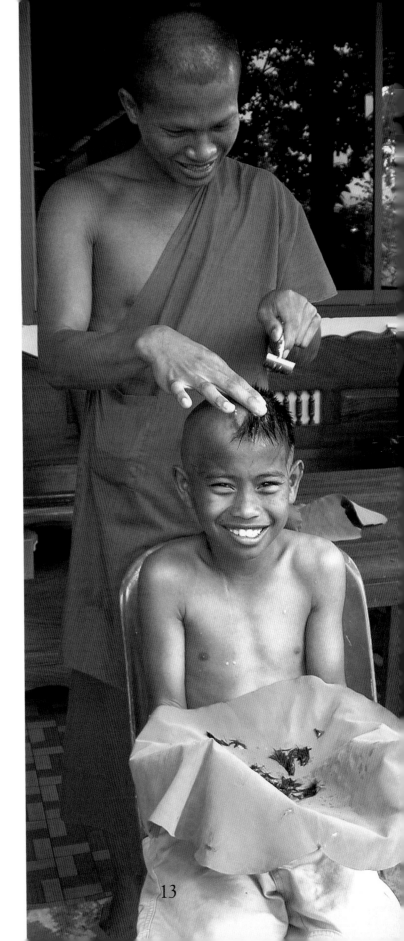

The boys dress in white. We all go to a bigger temple nearby. The boys walk around the temple **chanting** and carrying gifts for the monks.

The ceremony begins. We watch from the back of the temple. The head monk tells the boys what their duties will be. He tells them he will be their teacher, he will give them food and shelter, and look after them if they are sick.

The boys dress in their robes. "I'll never be able to do this by myself," Baan says.

Head monk Charoen smiles. "Don't worry. We will help you, and you will soon learn."

Now the boys become monks. They promise to obey the ten rules for young monks. This is the greatest moment of Baan's life.

The next day, at dawn, the boys begin the long walk to the village with the older monks. Baan feels every stone under his bare feet, and his stomach growls with hunger.

People in the village put rice into each monk's bowl. Back at the monastery, the monks share their food with the older monks and visitors.

19

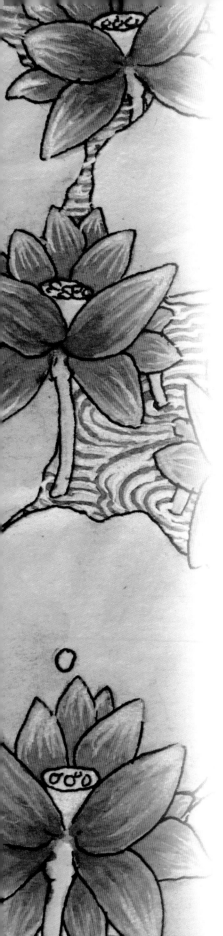

Baan enjoys his lessons from head monk Charoen.

"The Buddha was a rich prince named **Siddhartha**. When he was 16 he left his life of **luxury** to try to find the real meaning of life.

He lived a simple life and thought deeply until the meaning of life came to him.

This understanding was called **enlightenment** and he became the Buddha or 'enlightened one'."

The monks sleep on mats on the floor of their huts. They wake long before dawn and **meditate** by candlelight. After their walk to the village they are very hungry. Breakfast is important as the monks cannot eat anything after midday. They can drink at any time.

After breakfast there are jobs to be done, but everyone stops to listen to Baan's story.

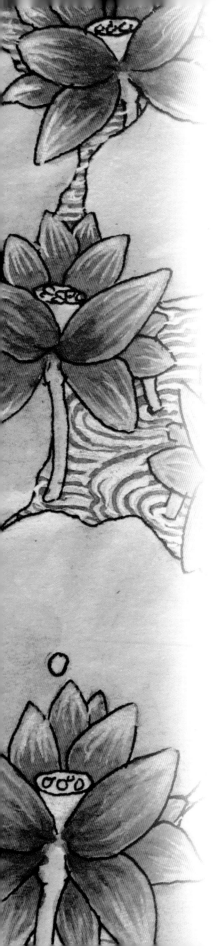

Baan and his friends spend hours every day meditating and chanting. Baan learns how to empty his mind and think good and peaceful thoughts.

24

The peace of the monastery is broken when the boys tumble into the water for a long bath at the end of each hot day. Head monk Charoen smiles as they dip, swing, and duck in the cool water.

Monk Lek often takes the boys for walks in the countryside. He tells them about the times he left the monastery to wander and live like the Buddha did. Baan loves to hear his stories of sleeping in the jungle. "Perhaps next year you could come with me," says monk Lek.

Back at the monastery, Baan fetches water from the rainwater tank. Now he knows how the monks use all the buckets they are given. He remembers that the Buddha said, "Drop by drop, the water pot is filled. A little at a time, wise people make themselves good."

27

Baan wakes up early on his last morning at the monastery. He is sad to leave, but happy to go home.

At the leaving ceremony the young monks bow in front of the Buddha's statue. Head monk Charoen pulls the robe off each monk's shoulder and they become just boys again.

"Pa, it's good to be home but I know I'll go back.
I want to learn more about Buddhism," says Baan.
I laugh. "Yes, but you are an ordinary boy now.
Take the water buffalo for a bath. Be quick.
Someone special is coming to celebrate."
Baan hears a familiar voice. Could it be his
mother, come all the way home from Bangkok?

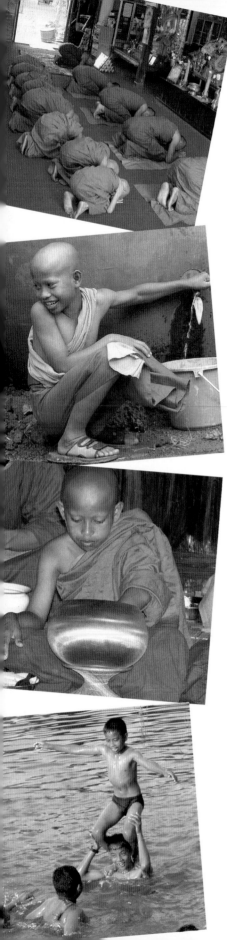

Notes for parents and teachers

Buddhism started in India about 2,500 years ago. It follows the teachings of a man called Siddhartha Gautama, who later became the Buddha, meaning 'enlightened one.' Today, Buddhism has over 400 million followers, and the religion has spread from Asia as far as Europe and the U.S.A.

Pages 6 and 7

In Thailand, you can become a monk for just a short time if you wish. Some people are monks for a week, some for several months or years, and some for a lifetime. Monks are more likely to achieve enlightenment than others because they have given up an ordinary life in the hope of gaining wisdom and purification.

Page 8

Buddhists gain merit by doing good deeds. By helping the monks, Baan is gaining merit. Gaining merit is like collecting good points for this life and the next. This is the Buddhist law of cause and effect, known as *karma*.

Buddhism teaches that lives do not begin with birth and end with death, but carry on for many lifetimes. Each time something dies, it is reincarnated as something else. If we lead a good life this time, our next life will be even better. However, if we lead a bad life, our next one will be harsh. We may not even be reborn as a human. This cycle of rebirth is called *samsara*.

Page 12

When the boys touch the ground three times with their heads, this represents the Triple Gem. This is the Buddha, the *Dharma* (the teachings of the Buddha), and the *Sangha* (the community of monks and nuns).

Page 14

At the temple, or *wat,* the boys line up to walk around the outside three times. They chant as they walk, contemplating the Triple Gem: the Buddha, his teachings, and the monks. Their families and friends also chant as they follow them around. Their grandparents carry the few possessions the boys are allowed to own

30

once they are monks. These include a set of robes, an umbrella, a bowl, a razor, string for holding up their robes if necessary, a cup, and a filter to stop the monks from accidentally killing an insect by swallowing it. Monks must not kill anything, not even a worm or a flower.

Page 17

The novice monks have to follow ten training rules. These forbid stealing, lying, drinking alcohol, physical pleasure, eating after midday, listening to music, dancing, wearing jewelry, sleeping on high beds, and accepting or handling money.

Pages 18 and 19

Back at the monastery, women serve the food on big trays that are passed to the monks first. As the grandfather of a monk, Baan's grandfather is given the honor of serving the trays to the monks. After the monks have taken as much food as they need, the content of the trays is given to the villagers who are present.

For the older monks this is the only meal of the day. The younger monks, such as Baan and his friends, are able to eat until midday but must not eat anything between noon and breakfast the next day. They are allowed to drink whenever they are thirsty.

Pages 20 and 21

Once he had found the path to enlightenment, the Buddha spent the next 45 years teaching his followers how to achieve enlightenment or *Nirvana*, a state of bliss and perfect peace. Anyone can do this, but it may take several lifetimes. To do this, Buddhists try to follow the five precepts, or moral rules, that were laid down by the Buddha. These rules say that people cannot kill, steal, lie, have physical pleasures, drink alcohol, or take drugs.

Buddhists can also work toward enlightenment by following the eight-fold path, which is neatly summed up in a verse told by the Buddha to his followers: "To refrain from all evil, to do what is good, to cleanse one's mind. This is the advice to all.'"

The Buddha taught that people could free themselves from suffering by accepting the situation they are in and following the four noble truths, which are:
- Life is filled with difficulties and suffering.
- The cause of suffering is craving the wrong things.
- It is possible to find an end to suffering.
- The Buddha can teach the way to end suffering.

31

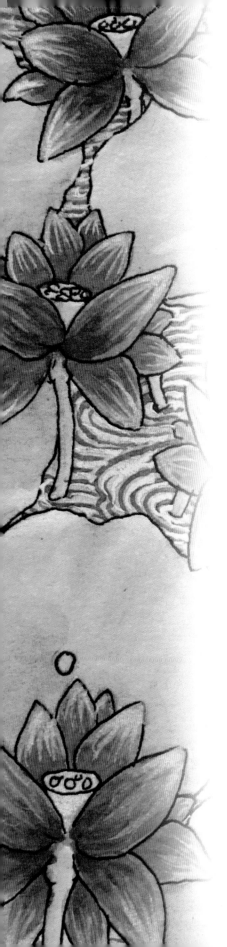

Glossary

Buddha The man who started Buddhism
Buddhist A person who follows the religion of Buddhism
chant To sing words over and over
enlightenment Understanding the meaning of life and living happily
lotus A plant that grows in water. It is important to Buddhists
luxury Having expensive and special belongings that are not necessary
meditate Thinking deeply about something
monastery The place where a group of monks or nuns live
monk A man or boy who has devoted himself to the Buddha and his teachings
offering A gift given to monks to help them
Siddhartha The name of the prince who became the Buddha

Index

Printed in China—CT